JKJC

W9-BIW-694

dabble lab

10-MINUTE
CRAFTY
PROJECTS

BY ELSIE OLSON

CAPSTONE PRESS
a capstone imprint

Dabble Lab is published by Capstone Press, a Capstone imprint.
1710 Roe Crest Drive, North Mankato, Minnesota 56003
capstonepub.com

Library of Congress Cataloging-in-Publication Data
Names: Olson, Elsie, 1986- author.
Title: 10-minute crafty projects / by Elsie Olson.
Description: North Mankato : Capstone Press, a Capstone imprint, [2022] | Series: 10-minute makers | Includes bibliographical references. | Audience: Ages 8-11 | Audience: Grades 4-6 | Summary: "Kids will be making in no time with this collection of easy 10-minute crafty projects that are perfect for makerspaces, including container garlands, string art designs, glitter jars, and more"– Provided by publisher.
Identifiers: LCCN 2021029671 | ISBN 9781663959041 (hardcover) | ISBN 9781666322170 (pdf) | ISBN 9781666322194 (kindle edition)
Subjects: LCSH: Handicraft for children–Juvenile literature.
Classification: LCC TT160 .O476 2022 | DDC 745.5083–dc23
LC record available at https://lccn.loc.gov/2021029671

Image Credits
Project photos: Mighty Media, Inc.
Liz Salzmann, p. 16 (dog)

Design Elements
Shutterstock Images

Editorial Credits
Editor: Liz Salzmann
Production Specialist: Aruna Rangarajan

TABLE OF CONTENTS

GOT 10 MINUTES?

Clean out your backpack, junk drawer, and locker. Then get crafty and put those odds and ends to good use! In 10 minutes or less, you can make a wind chime, a disco ball, and more. The best part? These quick and easy projects will leave you with loads of time to clean up when you're finished!

General Supplies and Tools

buttons   scissors
chenille stems   soda bottle
duct tape   straws
hot glue gun   string
keys
magnets
rubber bands

Tips

- Before starting a project, read the instructions. Then gather the supplies and tools you'll need.

- These crafty projects are about being creative with stray bits and pieces. You might not have all the materials shown in a project, and that's OK! Just substitute the odds and ends you can find.

- Make sure to get permission before using odds and ends in these projects.

- Ask an adult to help you with sharp or hot tools.

- Change things up! Don't be afraid to make these projects your own.

CONTAINER GARLAND

Upcycle empty plastic tubs into a colorful garland!
Hang it above your bed or in your doorway.

What You Need:

- small plastic tubs
- pen
- duct tape
- chenille stems
- ruler
- scissors
- string

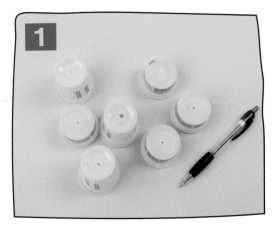

What You Do:

1 Use a pen to poke a hole through the bottom of each tub.

2 Decorate the tubs by wrapping them with colorful duct tape.

3 Cut a piece of chenille stem for each tub. Make each piece 3 to 4 inches (7.5 to 10 centimeters) long.

4 Push both ends of a stem piece through the hole in a tub. Bend back the ends inside the tub to hold the stem in place. The loop should be outside the tub. Repeat with each tub.

5 Cut a length of string several feet long. Tie the tubs to the string so they are several inches apart. Hang up your art!

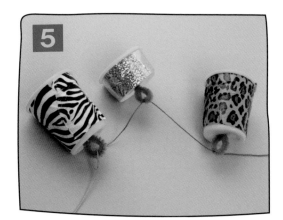

TIP If your tubs are too thick to poke a pen through, try a nail or craft knife instead.

7

STEAMPUNK MAGNET

Does your fridge need a little flair? Have no fear!
Steampunk magnets are here! Turn metal odds
and ends into a dynamic decoration.

What You Need:

small metal objects, such as washers, springs, gears & screws (make sure they will stick to the magnet)

hot glue gun

magnet

What You Do:

1 Create an interesting arrangement using several metal objects.

2 Glue the objects together to form a cluster.

3 Stick a magnet on the back of the cluster. Then stick the magnet on a refrigerator or other metal surface!

TIP Make more clusters of objects. Since the magnet is not glued on, you can switch clusters whenever you want!

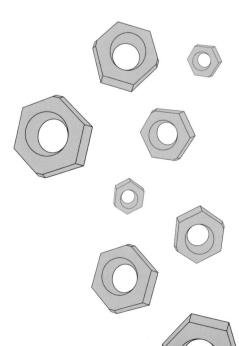

RUBBER BAND CUFF

Rubber bands come in all shapes, sizes, and colors.
Dig into your desk and give some old rubber bands
new life with this stylish cuff.

What You Need:

small plastic soda bottle

craft knife

ruler

scissors

rubber bands

What You Do:

1 Carefully use a craft knife to cut a ring out of the bottle. The ring should be about 1 inch (2.5 cm) wide.

2 Cut across the ring so it can open to fit around your wrist.

3 Wrap rubber bands around the ring. Alternate colors to make a pattern.

TIP Save rubber bands from bunches of fruits and vegetables for different sizes and textures!

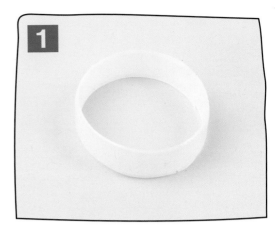

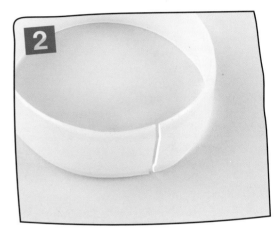

BUTTON ART

Buttons, buttons everywhere! Collect old or stray buttons to create an amazing mosaic design.

What You Need:

corkboard, cardboard, or canvas

marker

buttons in different shapes, sizes & colors

hot glue gun

What You Do:

1 Draw your design on the corkboard or other surface.

2 Arrange buttons on top of the design until it is completely covered.

3 Glue the buttons in place. Then display your picture somewhere you can admire it!

TIP Think of creative ways to use a button's round shape in your design. For example, white buttons make perfect air bubbles!

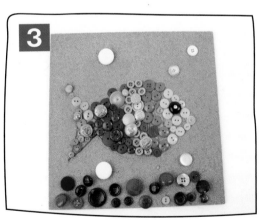

13

UNDERCOVER GLASSES

Plastic sunglasses are common giveaways at parades, fairs, and other events. Turn an old pair of sunglasses into a top-secret disguise!

What You Need:

plastic sunglasses

Ping-Pong ball

craft knife

scissors

craft foam

pom-poms

craft glue

duct tape

hot glue gun

gems (optional)

What You Do:

1 Pop the sunglass lenses out of their frames.

2 Use the craft knife to carefully cut the Ping-Pong ball in half.

3 Cut shapes, such as a mustache or eyebrows, out of craft foam.

4 Cut apart pom-poms to make hair. Use craft glue to attach the hair to the craft foam shapes.

5 Cover one half of the Ping-Pong ball with duct tape. Hot glue it to the bottom of the glasses to make a nose. Use hot glue to attach the other shapes you made. Add gems if desired.

MARKER CAP FRAME

Old, dried out markers bumming you out?
Not anymore! Recycle colorful caps to make a
one-of-a-kind frame for your favorite photo!

What You Need:

4 paint stir sticks

hot glue gun

marker caps

tape

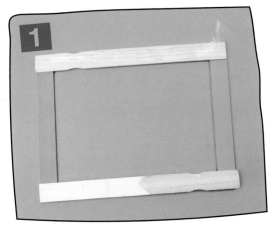

What You Do:

1 Arrange the stir sticks to make ta square or rectangle.

2 Glue the corners together to make a frame.

3 Glue marker caps around the frame until it is covered.

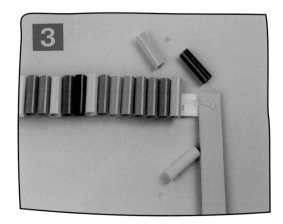

4 Tape a photo to the back of the frame.

TIP No markers? No problem! Substitute pieces of colored pencils, crayons, or any other colorful art supply.

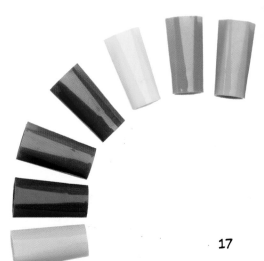

THUMBTACK DISCO BALL

Need a little sparkle in your day? This disco ball should do the trick! Hang this tennis-ball-turned-decoration anywhere you need a little shine.

What You Need:

string
ruler
scissors
thumbtacks

tennis ball
gems
hot glue gun
craft knife (optional)

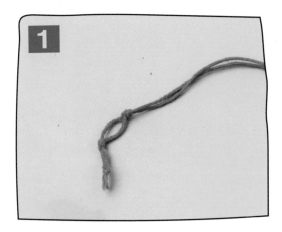

What You Do:

1 Cut a length of string about 6 inches (15 cm) long. Tie the ends together. Tie a second knot near the first so there is a small loop between the knots.

2 Push a thumbtack through the small loop and into the tennis ball.

3 Push more thumbtacks into the tennis ball until it is partially covered.

4 Hot glue gems onto the tennis ball until it has as much sparkle as you want!

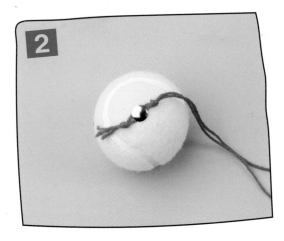

TIP It can be hard to push the thumbtacks into the tennis ball. Try using a craft knife to cut slits in the ball. Squeeze the ball to open the slits. Push a thumbtack through each slit!

19

NAME GAME COLLAGE

Do you have 99 pieces of a 100-piece puzzle?
Put pieces from incomplete puzzles and games
to use in a decoration that screams YOU!

What You Need:

cardboard or thick card stock

pencil

scissors

craft glue

foam brush

old puzzle & game pieces

What You Do:

1 Draw your initials or other letters on the cardboard. Cut them out.

2 Use a foam brush to cover a letter with craft glue.

3 Scatter the puzzle pieces across the glue. Arrange them so the letter is covered.

4 Brush glue on the other letter. Cover it with more puzzle pieces, or use play money or other game pieces.

TIP For a tidier look, trim any pieces that extend outside the edges of the letters.

21

MINI GLITTER SCENE

Glitter jars can help you calm yourself down. Turn a small jar into a calming scene. Then turn it over and back. Take a deep breath as you watch the glitter settle.

What You Need:

- paper & printer or drawing supplies
- tissue paper
- scissors
- small jar with lid
- clear craft glue
- craft foam
- hot glue gun
- small figurine
- measuring spoons
- glitter
- clear dish soap
- water

What You Do:

1. Think of the scene you want to create. Draw or print a small image for the scene. Cut other scene pieces out of tissue paper.

2. Turn the jar upside down. Glue the scene pieces to the outside of the jar. Make sure the images face the inside of the jar!

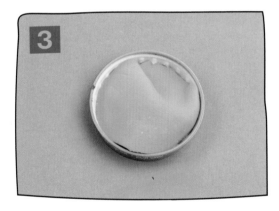

3. Cut a circle of craft foam a bit larger than the lid. Hot glue the circle inside the lid so it makes a hill in the middle. Hot glue the figurine on top of the hill.

4. Put 1 tablespoon (15 milliliters) of glitter and ¼ teaspoon (1.2 mL) of dish soap in the jar. Fill the jar with water, leaving a little space at the top.

5. Screw the lid on the jar. Set the jar down and watch the glitter float through the scene.

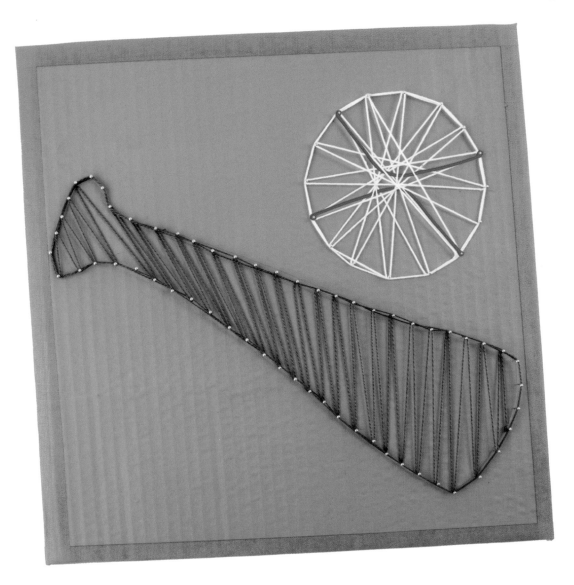

STRING ART

Bring some retro style to your bedroom or locker by creating your favorite things in string!

What You Need:

cardboard

pencil

straight pins

ruler

string

scissors

colored tape (optional)

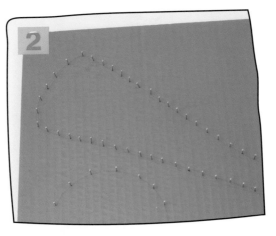

What You Do:

1 Draw the outline of a simple design on a piece of cardboard.

2 Stick pins into the outline. Space them about ½ inch (1.3 cm) apart.

3 Tie the string to one of the pins.

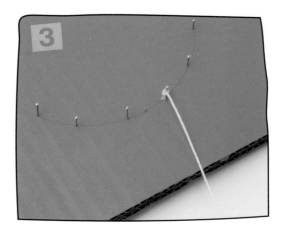

4 Run the string back and forth over the design, looping around each pin.

5 Wrap the string around the outside of the pins. Tie the string to a pin and trim the string.

6 Repeat steps 3 through 5 with other colors of string on other areas of your design.

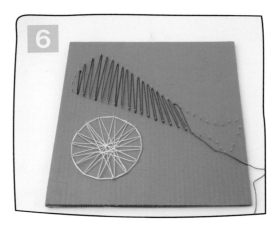

TIP Add a border to your art by sticking tape around the edges of the cardboard.

RIBBON GARLAND

Birthdays and other celebrations often end with a pile of gift wrap, ribbons, and bows. Turn these party leftovers into a party decoration!

What You Need:

ribbon

yarn

ruler

scissors

string

bells & feathers (optional)

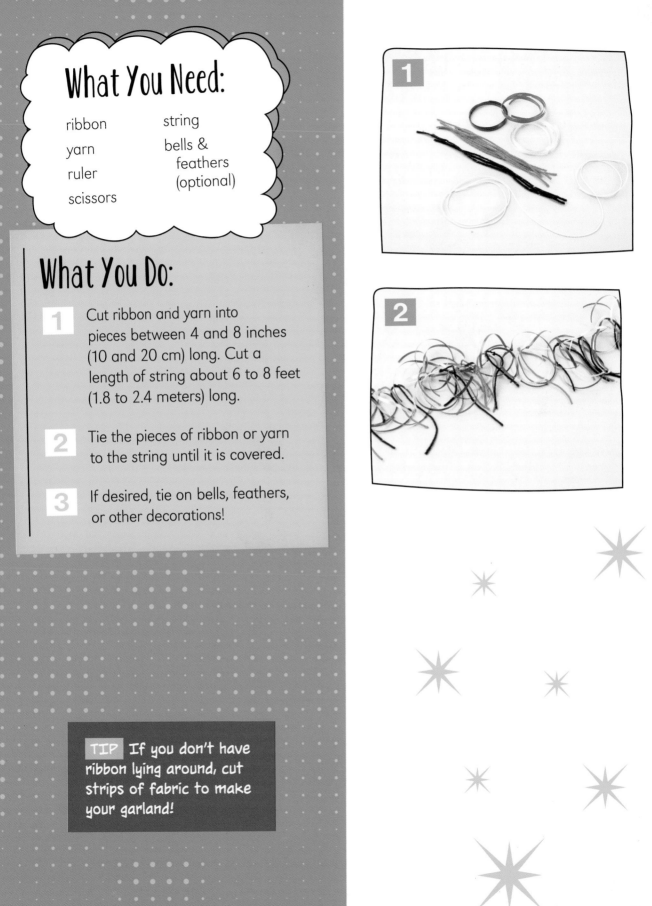

What You Do:

1 Cut ribbon and yarn into pieces between 4 and 8 inches (10 and 20 cm) long. Cut a length of string about 6 to 8 feet (1.8 to 2.4 meters) long.

2 Tie the pieces of ribbon or yarn to the string until it is covered.

3 If desired, tie on bells, feathers, or other decorations!

TIP If you don't have ribbon lying around, cut strips of fabric to make your garland!

PENCIL ORGANIZER

Unused drinking straws make the perfect organizer
for your desk or homework space!

What You Need:

round container

waxed paper

tape

drinking straws

scissors

hot glue gun

craft foam

What You Do:

1 Wrap a piece of waxed paper around the container. Tape it in place along the seam.

2 Cut straws into different lengths. They should all be longer than the container's height.

3 Glue the straw pieces to the waxed paper around the container.

4 Remove the container. Trim the extra waxed paper above the straws, leaving a cylinder made of straws.

5 Cut a circle of craft foam the size of the container's bottom. Glue it to the bottom of the straw cylinder.

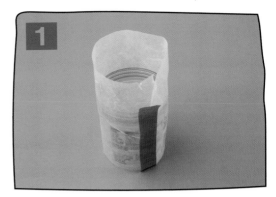

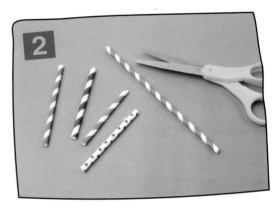

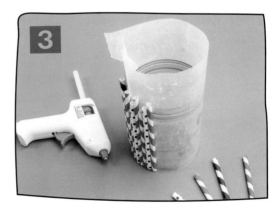

STRAW AND KEY WIND CHIME

Hang metal pieces in the breeze where they can jingle and jangle.

What You Need:

- 5 to 7 metal drinking straws
- string
- ruler
- scissors
- round shower curtain ring
- metal objects, such as keys, springs, key rings & more
- wire
- paint & paintbrush (optional)

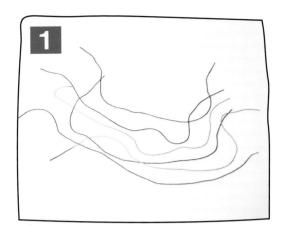

What You Do:

1 Cut a piece of string for each straw. The strings should each be about 1 foot (0.3 m) long.

2 Tie one end of a piece of string to the shower curtain ring. Thread the other end through a metal object and then through a straw.

3 Tie on other metal objects, such as springs, key rings, or keys.

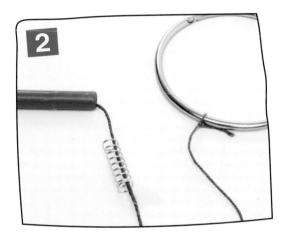

4 Repeat steps 2 and 3 to add the other strings. Space them evenly around the shower curtain ring.

5 Cut a piece of wire about 10 inches (25 cm) long. Twist the ends around the shower curtain ring on opposite sides. Use the wire to hang your wind chime.

TIP Paint the metal objects before connecting them. This will add extra color to your wind chime!

Read More

Kuskowski, Alex. *Cool Refashioned Hardware: Fun & Easy Fashion Projects*. Minneapolis: Abdo Publishing, 2016.

McLeod, Kimberly. *Fun and Easy Crafting with Recycled Materials: 60 Cool Projects that Reimagine Paper Rolls, Egg Cartons, Jars and More!* Salem, MA: Page Street Publishing Co., 2019.

Uliana, Kim. *Crafting Fun for Kids of All Ages: Pipe Cleaners, Paint & Pom-Poms Galore, Yarn & String & a Whole Lot More*. New York: Sky Pony Press, 2017.

Internet Sites

Country Living: 15 Easy Crafts for Kids That Will Brighten Up Rainy Days
countryliving.com/diy-crafts/g4988/easy-crafts-for-kids/

Parents: Kid Crafts
parents.com/fun/arts-crafts/kid/

The Spruce Crafts: Easy, 10-Minute Crafts for Kids
thesprucecrafts.com/10-minute-crafts-for-kids-1250670